Chase Your Dreams Never Give Up!

Written By

Elina Salajeva

Touchladybirdlucky Studios
A David Gomadza Production.
Elina Salajeva have asserted their rights under Copyright, Designs and Patents Act 1988 to be identified as the author of this work.
ISBN: 978-1-9164397-5-7
[Touchladybirdlucky Studios]
ISBN: 978-1539713135
[Createspace]
Copyright © 2016 Elina Salajeva.
All rights reserved.

DEDICATION

To my family, especially my grandmother, my mum, my dad and my sister Ewa, who have been of great support and to David who has been a source of great inspiration.

Lots of love.

ACKNOWLEDGMENTS

Many thanks and best wishes to the Elinadeivid brand. Big thanks also to Touchladybirdlucky Studios.

Chase Your Dreams Never Give Up!

Life is about taking risks, making new challenges, going for what you want in life, believing you are one of the few destined for glory, it's going beyond the ordinary, it's about being focused, determined, disciplined and resilient and having that ambition, that drive and willpower to AIM and ACHIEVE glory.
What are you waiting for?
Take the Challenge TODAY!
Achieve greatness!

Aim Higher In The End It Will Pay Off

Clearly define your goals, work hard and remain focused, determined and resilient, in the end you have great rewards.

OVERVIEW

Have you ever wondered what life would be like if you were to make your dreams come true? Just imagine living that lifestyle you have ever wanted, having a great job, a great career, looking fabulous, feeling great about yourself, or just setting up that successful business you have ever wished you had. Or ask yourself this question,

"What can I change today to make my dreams come true?" What can I change today to have a better lifestyle and what can I change today to look and feel fabulous? If you are to change something today, to have a better job, to have a successful business, to look fantastic and feel great about yourself what would it be?

Have you ever tried to start something for instance, an online business and ended up giving up? Have you ever tried to change your lifestyle, to change your career or get a new job, to change how you look and feel and tried to change what you eat and ended up back to where you were before?

Have you failed before? Were you faced with a lot of obstacles that in the end you just gave up? Chase your dreams and never give up is the key to your success. It's that willingness and inner drive to keep on going, to push for what you want, to fight for what you want to be and stand up and work hard for how you want to feel in face of all kinds of difficulties and obstacles and never giving up. Today is that day to take the challenge and achieve greatness. Take that challenge today, make the first step in fulfilling your dreams and achieving what

Elina Salajeva

you have ever wanted to achieve. If you have failed in the past, let that not discourage you, this book has the answers. Ever wanted to take that challenge and you were put off by lack of information and practical detailed guidelines? Then this book will be useful to you. Today is the day to say Yes! Action now! This book provides practical solutions and methods that can work. This book is your holy grail, inside you will find detailed methods and solutions, many suggestions to solve any glitches you might encounter later, and the book has plenty real-life examples.

This book will motivate and kick start that inner drive to see you achieve your dreams be it a new business, a better job, a new career, a better high self-esteemed lifestyle or that looking-great body and it doesn't stop there the book is full of guidelines, suggestions, numerous ideas for one to continually improve and maintain what has already been achieved without relapsing. The main problem is that after a while of working hard to get that new look for instances we as humans we tend to get back to our comfort zone and over time that dream, that goal is lost again, we go back to our comfort zone and accept that that's our destiny when in actual fact, that won't be true. We can be what we want to be we must aim higher and work towards that goal persistently.

There is a need today to change your lifestyle, you are not happy about your job or just want a new challenge then take action now. There are different problems hindering progress, stopping you from chasing your dreams, you lack the self-drive, that inspiration to make you want to be great, make you want to crave for success, these problems come in different forms, it could be your personal beliefs, it could be a lack of facilities and support in your local area, it could be a lack of information and practical solutions to your problems, or just your lack of that inner burning fire, that hunger for success enough to drive you and make you to take the challenge. Are these problems making you go in circles and making you miss out on things which you genuinely believe you would otherwise have enjoyed if you had achieved your goal. You could be having problems of self-esteem and lacking the Waal factor when you look yourself in the mirror. You could easily be failing to socialize just because you are overweight. You could be missing out on other things which you genuinely believe you would otherwise have enjoyed if you were not overweight.

CHAPTER ONE

This book provides practical solutions hints and tips to solve problems like dead-end jobs or just the need to improve your lifestyle. If you have a job but feel you can aim higher and get a better job, this book provides practical solutions and workable methods that can be tried to achieve that. This book provides practical ideas of taking control of yourself and finding happiness and self-esteem. Step-by-step methods to improve communication networks and boost your self-esteem.

The first step is the undoubted self-conviction that first there is a problem with the current situation. One must genuinely believe that the current situation is unworkable, and a solution is needed. First step is to identify and highlight that a problem exists. Once the problem is identified and circled the second step is to highlight what one is missing out on certain things a, b, c etc. for example due to the problem. There is a causal-effect phenomenon, because of the current situation for example this person is not having a, b, c, etc., and because of current situation one is missing out on this and that. It is because of current situation that one for instance, has low self-esteem and because of that low self-esteem one tends to avoid social gatherings for instance, which in turn makes things even worse because it becomes a vicious cycle, the lack of social inclusion in one's life heighten the problem. One must genuinely believe that a problem exists and because of this one is missing on life because of the problem. If it wasn't for the problem one would be enjoying a, b, c etc.

For example, your job might be taking a lot of your time and that the rewards are not so great. One could sacrifice one or two things and find a good job probably somewhere else and gain more rewards not just in terms of money but also in terms of time to spend with loved ones, or take a hobby or run the dog. Once that self-conviction is engraved in one's mind, and heart and with no doubt one acknowledges that there is a problem and something need to be done then and only then can one genuinely take the action and try to do something about it. Everyone would want a great life, a great job, a successful business, everyone wants to feel good and look great but it takes more than just intelligent to achieve one's dreams. It requires a great deal of commitment and dedication, one must have the stamina and energy to keep on going and never giving up. Nevertheless, they say where there is a will there is always a way, this book is the answer, all you want is within your reach. It can be achieved but I'm not saying it's a walk in the park, but with the right recipe, the right inner drive, energy and determination it's all achievable.

Start that challenge Today! Action Today! See yourself achieve great things, see that new look, feel that energy emanating from that glowing high esteemed mind of yours. All you must say is YES to yourself, convince yourself that you want this change, say YES you want this new life, say YES you want this life then all will fall into place. Look in the mirror, make that fist, punch the air and say YES! I want this change. I want this new look. I want this better life style. I want this new business. YES! I want this new job. YES! I want this new image whatever you are dreaming of achieving, it's that self-conviction, that acknowledgment that you genuinely want this which will see you through. Say YES I can end this vicious cycle say YES I can start something new, a new life, I can take control of myself, I can be better and I believe it's achievable.

Elina Salajeva

Once one is convinced that there is a problem it will be easy to take the challenge otherwise lack of this self-conviction will make one lose interest after few days of trying or even weeks, because that inner drive, that hunger for success will be lacking within.

This acknowledgment incites or stimulates that inner drive for one to be a better person and for one to achieve greatness. There are some traits that will help one achieve what they want, not everyone is born with these but the good news is that they can be inherited through careful practice and learning.

WRITE DOWN ANY IDEAS AND PLANS AS YOU GO.

1.

2.

3.

4.

5.

6.

7.

8.

9.

10.

CHAPTER TWO

Just like a soldier, stay focused be persistent, diligent, courageous, motivated and disciplined.

Follow clearly defined practices and methods, you must be consistent courageous fearless, highly motivated and disciplined as well, in other words think like a soldier you should be able to stay focused until task at hand is achieved. Follow clearly defined methods of achieving that goal. Think like a leader be as independent and self-sufficient. You need some leadership skills you should be able to be the center piece in the decision-making process you should be able to lead yourself, make concrete decisions, be persistent in whatever you do, take no for an answer and don't procrastinate. To succeed, one must think independently, you should view yourself as the sole entity, you are the main man, you are the center of focus and life should revolve around you.

I recall my cat Persiks up to all kinds of mischievousness all day but one thing that was for sure with him, was that he saw himself as independent and self-sufficient, he was free to make his own moves, he wasn't dependent on me, he stuck around only because he wanted to, it was never because of the scrumptious fish dishes I made him, no, it was simply because he saw it beneficial to him to stick around.

I remember one morning my cat Persiks, got up, jumped on my bed and laid down next to me, he laid down there for some time. I took my hand and started rubbing his fur, for some time he looked relaxed. "Oh Persik, what are you up to!" I remarked getting up and going to make a good meal for him. He followed me, stood there for some time sniffed the food and the next minute he was gone. He went for hours leaving my delicious fish dish untouched.

In life, we humans must try to live fruitful lives, don't get in the habit of following routine, possibly boring life styles, create opportunities, don't just stick around just because it's your comfort zone, set new goals, take opportunities be it business wise or job opportunities. Try to be independent in decision making and financially.

Just like cats have a good relationship with the people you know. Strive to maintain sound relationships with friends, colleagues and other potentially helpful people who contribute to your success. Minimize or strive to eliminate relationship that aren't beneficial where the other party drains your resources financially and time wise. Maintain healthy relationships where you are all equal partners where you benefit as well where you learn something beneficial to your development and success. Have abundant self-drive and high self-esteem. You are the first focus, just like my cat Persik, lick yourself first, put your house in order first, you are the one on top of the pyramid. Be smart and lick yourself before licking others. You are first point; a cat can lick itself for hours. Image is everything, strive to be the best, strive to be the center of admiration, abundant knowledge, and skills together with practical solutions to problems.

Strive to be the one, people turn to for advice and resolutions, try to be the disputes solver. Be fair but strict and command the respect of others. These attributes or qualities cannot be obtained overnight if you were born without these, then learn and acquire these through learning and putting everything to practice. Strive to maintain very good relationship with friends, colleagues and potentially other successful people who can or might contribute enormously to your development and success.

Share information and advice and work together as a team. If you are the leader, then know everyone's weaknesses and strengths.

CHAPTER THREE

Strive to maintain good relationships with friends and colleagues.

Take all necessary steps to make sure you feel fabulous about yourself. Persiks my cat doesn't leave any fur not licked, he licks himself until he feels he is the "Cat main man likewise to be successful in whatever you do, you should aim to be admired, aim to be a leader strive to have followers people who can look up to you. Be adaptable and easily adjust to changing factors.

Chase Your Dreams Never Give Up!

Strive to adjust to changing influences quickly you should be able to take opportunities whether business or job opportunities quickly.

Reacting and adjusting to opportunities can be the main factor determining the success or failure of a business or the ability to achieve one's goals, be it a change in life style or a new job or a new career or just feeling good about oneself.

Be thorough and tough but overall be fair and be predictable I recall my grandma one day telling me that sweetness doesn't pay and over the years observing my cat Persik has reinforced this notion. Sweetness is for the ordinary average people, the kinds of people who just go with the flow, people who don't have the self-drive to aim higher, people who accept the current norms, people who think that what they have is what they are destined to have in life.

Ambitious people, people who dream of great things, people who want to be in control of their lives, people who want what's best for them are like cats, they don't detect sweetness, sweetness cannot be detected by their whiskers, these people have no time to be sweet to everyone, these people are tough, they know sweetness doesn't pay, they put tough guidelines and follow these through, they put plans in place and follow these. Sweetness is common among humans but it's an opportunity cost in terms of time and resources, being sweet to others means a cost in terms of resources financially and in terms of time. Whether it's a business or job, stick around only if it's beneficial to you, stick only if it makes sense.

WRITE DOWN ANY IDEAS AND PLANS AS YOU GO.

1.

2.

3.

Strive to be the center of attention, skills and admiration.

Chase Your Dreams Never Give Up!

To succeed weigh everything in monetary terms, time you spend being sweet to others where benefits to you are minimal that's an opportunity cost you could be doing something that is useful to your growth and development. See yourself as the leader your own boss don't be sweet but be just and reasonable and try to be predictable in whatever you do.

Make sound decisions based on facts and always provide solutions. If things are not going well complain, point to the problem don't be shy. Say things as they are don't let feelings cloud your judgment, just like a cat if you don't want to eat jellyfish stand up and highlight the issue demand better things.

WRITE DOWN ANY IDEAS AND PLANS AS YOU GO.

1.
2.
3.
4.
5.
6.
7.
8.
9.
10.

CHAPTER FOUR

You need to be aggressive to some extent to command the respect of others and their loyalty as in the long run people around you will see that your decisions are in their interest, as well as your business, in the future as you succeed they will see the benefits of your decisions hence offering protection in terms of jobs and income. Even if it's about changing your lifestyle people will see a new you, they will look up to you and you will command their respect as well, they will see you as a role model.

Make decisions based on facts and be in control all the time. If life has become routine immediately seek to provide workable solutions and don't hesitates to change things regardless of other people's feelings. Life is making changes and be in control, always try to bring a new sense of direction and confidence. Try to make decisions based on the bigger picture. Make tough decisions be energetic and strong willed. Be as bold as possible competitive and welcome challenges and continuously try to improve or change things.

WRITE DOWN ANY IDEAS AND PLANS AS YOU GO.

1.

2.

3.

Be the boss, the leader, be self-sufficient and independent.

CHAPTER FIVE

Work well with others and share information.

Learn from mistakes develop intelligent skills and methods to solve day-to-day problems.

Take the center stage, be the center of knowledge skills and admiration be honest always no need for tricks, strive to be just and honest and aim to be trusted and respected. Normally don't depend on emotions you must be cold sometimes domineering and self-sufficient. Try not to rely on others although you work well with others you aim to provide everything you need yourself.

Chase Your Dreams Never Give Up!

Never give up, think like a cat always get what you want, be self-sufficient independent and persistent. If you want results Never give up chase your dreams. Always think like a cat to dominate if you had the chance and if need be, then you must take all your opponents out, be competitive.

The key to success is being as persistent as a cat, never give up, life is full of surprises and challenges too many obstacles to overcome, one must be thick skinned to achieve and excel. Have you ever come across a hungry cat, when he or she wants food, he will growl he will cry continuous, the more you don't act quickly the more he becomes louder and louder and there will come a stage if you don't respond he will start being aggressive to get your attention?

Like wise to succeed you need a strong heart, one must be determined to overcome anything coming your way to achieve that goal. They say first if you don't succeed then try again, and I say again and again, until you get results. Most of the time most people achieve results just, few moments before they were about to give up.

WRITE DOWN ANY IDEAS AND PLANS AS YOU GO.

1.

2.

3.

4.

5.

6.

CHAPTER SIX

Like Persik be as persistent as you can until the objective is achieved.

Like my cat Persiks the key to success is persistence, it takes more than just intelligence, it is the willingness to keep on going even in face of difficulties that brings about success. It is the ability to keep on working, researching, tinkering and improving that brings about great results. It is the continuous tinkering, or brain storming that will bring about the success in the future, be a die-hard, if it's a problem try different solutions, look at it from different angles, ask others for ideas look at it from someone else's perspective, then combined with your own views and try to come up with a solution.

You can learn from others look at other successful people and learn from them, see what they have done right, copy what is good and tailor others' successful methods to suit your own style or business but the key to riches is trying to be as original as possible. Look at it as there is always another better way of doings things which is waiting to be discovered.

Your motto should be let's do it now nothing impossible no fear always up for challenges. Don't be ambiguous be straight to the point don't be vague let everyone know what they are dealing with and be straight to the point so in turn you are respected and trusted and those around you will feel they can depend on you and they can trust and rely on you. Your decision should be based on facts gather relevant information about an issue at hand before passing judgment.

Be ready to start a task as soon as possible, aim to avoid wasting time and resources spend few but productive hours on tasks and spend more time relaxing and socializing.

Don't do everything yourself. Delegate and organize tasks for others. Let others do the routine tasks and you concentrate on important long-term goals. Most of the time think you are always right, although you might not be right, always it's that belief that you are right that help you make right decisions, it's that fear of making mistakes that builds your character. No room for mistakes learn from mistakes and make quick decisions based on experience and past knowledge or your gut instincts.

To be able to succeed, you must set clearly defined goals. State your objectives, know what you want to achieve and set achievable goals. Goal setting is key to any success, you must set tangible, achievable goals that can be measured in terms of time and results. Once you know what you want, then can you start working towards that. If it's a successful business, be it improved life style, be it a feel-good body and a healthy life style goal setting is of paramount importance. Visualize the benefits to be achieved and always project to that time in the future when you have achieved your goal to keep your mind on the ball.

WRITE DOWN ANY IDEAS AND PLANS AS YOU GO.

1.

2.

3.

CHAPTER SEVEN

It can be boring and frustrating waiting for one to achieve their goal, there are many obstacles, frustrations and things that can make you go off course and lose sight of what you are trying to achieve, therefore there is a need for continuous self-motivating oneself.

There is need to continuously instill interest in the project to remain on course when the tough gets going. Keep reminding yourself of what you what to achieve, instill that zeal you hard the first time you came up with this idea, remind yourself of the benefits you will achieve be it financial or emotional. Look at good examples, people who have already achieved what you are trying to achieve, let them be your source of inspiration and keep on track. Adjust to progress as you go along, speed up and slow down accordingly looking at deadlines and time frames. Be flexible easily adjust considering the current circumstances and when you are behind schedule, get more done.

When behind schedule get, more people involved, to keep up, put more time and when on track then slow down or reduce time you spend on your goal. Model your character to be a persistent person that way you won't quit easily when faced with obstacles.

Today is the day for you to take the challenge. Today is the day you put your ideas into action. Today is the day you say I want greatness, I want that successful business. I want that new career that new job. I want that fabulous lifestyle.

I want that new look or I want that great body or I want that healthy life style. Whatever it is its action Now! Make your dreams come true put your plans to paper, instill your ideas in your mind, be ambitious and highly motivated, engrave these in your veins and say I can do this. You must convince yourself first that this is what you want. It starts with you. Do you know what you want? Have you wasted time just thinking about this, have you spent years imagining this but without taking that first step?

Has fears in the past hindered you to start the challenge. In most cases let me tell you, it's not easy, but if you follow the advice and guidelines in this book I tell you this, your ideas, your dreams, your goals can be achieved. Its persistence that brings about results, its sheer determination and true to oneself that makes things happen. It's self-conviction that makes one realize their goals. It's that burning hunger, that cravenness to succeed, that passion to succeed that will drive one to achieve their goals.

You must convince yourself that this lifestyle you have now is OK but not for you. From my own experience, I think this is the thin line that determines success or failure. It's going beyond the current norm and accept that this is not your fate, you are destined for greater things but you just didn't know it. I think it's that sheer realization that you can achieve greatness that makes some people millionaires. It's denying that what you have is what you are destined to have, it's the simple realization and acceptance that OK what you have now is good lifestyle but in your capabilities, you can achieve better.

Success doesn't come over night but can be achieved if you follow defined procedures be it to make money through a business or to have a healthy living lifestyle. It's putting things in place and following those set goals and rules that brings about success. Most people have ideas and dreams and want to be millionaires they want healthy life styles they want to look great.

But for most it's just an idea, it's just a dream, it's just a wish nothing gets taken seriously, nothing is put on paper or ever tried, or when tried these are quickly abandoned and forgotten.

CHAPTER EIGHT

I had great ideas and great goals and when I start something, then after sometime I quickly abandon my goals and revert to my comfort zone. After a while I start thinking about my goals again, then I start researching and gathering information after some days or weeks of constantly on the ball then I revert to my old comfort zone.

Then for a while thing gets better be it money wise until that glitch again when ends don't meet then I start thinking about finding a project that brings real changes in my life. This is the vicious cycle associated with failure and the one that one need to overcome, it's not easy but I tell you that if you are following the advice in this book, you are certainly sure going to overcome this cycle and only then will you be able to cross that thin line that distinguish millionaires from the average people.

There comes my emphasis again that one must accept and convince him or herself that first that there is a problem, first that the current way of life isn't enough, first that this life style can be improved, or first just that one has a dream and want to achieve greatness. It is this current situation that makes one miss out on things life must offer, because of this situation ones aren't enjoying certain things and this deprivation help drive one to act, one to act and try to eliminate the problem or address the situation. Self-conviction is paramount to this process and only after that can one seriously do something about the current situation. It's not easy but achievable hence this book. Whatever it is its action now.

I challenge you to assess yourself and see if you can change something today, I challenge you to convince yourself that you want something better, to convince yourself that you can do better, to convince yourself that you can achieve greatness, after that self-conviction only and only then can I demand immediate action. This book will help and guide you in tried and tested methods and guidelines and plans you can follow to achieve whatever you want to achieve, be it more money through your own successful business, a new career or a new job or just improved self-esteem through looking fabulous or a healthy life style. I'm living proof that it takes more than intelligence and lucky to be successful in life and from my own experience there are other attributes that determines ones' failure or success and as I learned from my cat Persik, persistence is an often not talked about attribute that after reading this book you will realize that it takes more than just a few mew mews to be successful.

The methods proposed in this book if applied persistently in the end you are bound to realize your own goals. It's easy to follow they all fit in the place like a jigsaw puzzle. Therefore it is important to read stage by stage and apply the proposed methods in order as proposed because skipping some suggested methods will make other methods or later stages impracticable, for instance, the first stage is the self-conviction that one believes that there is a problem be it lack of enough money, be it boring routine lifestyles, be it feeling sluggish because you don't feel fabulous or you have a low self-esteem because of poor life style, or sheer realization that one is bound to achieve greatness.

It is this self-conviction and its realization and acceptance that will drive and motivate one to demand immediate action and follow the other steps to realize one's dream. It is this belief that will drive one to achieve their goal. It's this self-conviction that will motivate one to stay focused and on course to achieve ones' goals.

Without this belief and the realization that there is a problem it is easy to stop along the way and revert to one's comfort zone.

It's the instilling of that conviction in one's brain, in one's heart in one's veins in one's feelings that's of paramount importance and a sole determinant factor to whether one will embark on working towards that goal and staying focused. This also determines if one is to stay motivated and keep the fire burning

When one is sure that they want to be better, they want better lifestyles, better income, better images or just want new challenges only then can they move to the next stage of doing something about this? This should be taken seriously and something that should be done like today. Stand up, sign up and buy now whatever it is its action now. If you want this, then get it today.

This book will provide detailed and concrete methods and ideas that are workable. The methods in this book have been tried and tested and depending on what ones is trying to achieve if put in practice one's goals can be achieved. Just imagine successfully setting up an online fashion business you have been dreading to fail but after reading my book and being persistent and never giving up you finally made it. You have just made your first sales online and you are excited about this.

You have been trying for years and before they had been obstacles that made you start and stop but this time after reading my book you have realized that although you were doing the same things before and failing, this time you have realized that it's following the guidelines and proposed methods and putting these in practice continuously and persistently never giving up that now you have made your first sales.

For most people they have the knowledge of what to do but it's that guided help and methodology that they are lacking, for most people it's the lack of proper understanding what it actually take to succeed, they cut corners they want results fast that they skip other stages, they poorly plan things, they assume following a detailed plan and sticking to plans as advised in this book doesn't really matter but I say to you today that isn't correct, for example babies learn to walk after they have been crawling for some months. They can't learn to walk first before they crawl, likewise achieving success depends on completing the lower level stages first thoroughly before moving to upper level stages because what happens in later stages is dependent upon the successful completion and launching of the lower level stages.

If you skip the first stages or pay no particular attention to these, then there will problems later. A good example is when one doesn't convince him or herself that there is a problem that need resolving, for example, you are in a vicious cycle after a few months of working towards your goal then you become money less maybe because of more unexpected bills if you don't convince yourself that there is a problem and action needs to be taken then it will be difficult to try now and come up with another way of topping up your income.

Another example is when one has a low self-esteem he or she feels down and unwanted until he or she can admit that his or her self-esteem is low it will be difficult to convince him or herself that action need to be taken now to build that self-esteem in the long run. There must be real self-conviction for one to embark NOW and act to accentuate or eliminate the problem.

In most cases in such situations where one tries to skip other stages or not fully follow as advised in this book then there will be instances when after a few weeks or months it will be easy to give up and the whole thing abandoned.

Chase Your Dreams Never Give Up!

In this book I have put things in the place that one must follow to stay on track. In this book, it will be emphasized that every stage is crucial and in its own right, very important. One must take himself or herself to that time in the future when he or she has achieved his or her goals. In other words, one must visualize himself or herself as having already achieved the goal, bring the future to the present day, think as if you already have had the successful business, think as if you have already attained that high self-esteem and now you are feeling a million dollars, thinks as if you have already achieved that goddess or muscle body and you are just loving that new look.

Imagine what you would do if you had more money, high self-esteem and or just looking fantastic and let that be your drive to stay focused, read about other people who have achieved what you are trying to achieve now, associate yourself with people with similar goals. For example, one of the advised methods and attained attributes one should adopt is to look at your environment and its influence. Look at what has hindered you in the past in achieving this goal, are those factors still there, is it people you are associating yourself with and what can be done to alleviate the problem or eliminate it all.

If you go back to previous chapters of dos and don'ts, you will notice that I emphasized that sweetness doesn't pay. Be tough be strict if it means avoiding your current circle of friends so be it. If you want to build your self-esteem for example and you know your friend is going all the time to reduce you to nothing by name calling, so that he or she can feel better about him or herself at your expense, then it's time to say adios. Associate yourself with like-minded people, learn from already achievers. Work on all obstacles what I would encourage is to get a piece of paper divide it into two columns. Write the pros and the cons, ask yourself without getting into too much detail.

Write on the left half things you think and believe have hindered your progress or things you think will work against you achieving your goal. On the other half write down things you think will be beneficial to you to achieve your goal.

After listing all major obstacles and favorable then rate them giving marks out of ten for example, for each. For example, you want to go to the gym very often to boost your self-esteem so you feel good about yourself but you have a lazy friend he would rather drag you to the nearest pub anytime of the day, out of ten give this a mark according to how much influence he or she exerts. After looking at all factors then arrange these in order of importance as to how much this has influenced you, then take a strong approach if it means avoiding some people then take that step.

This book encourages a no-nonsense approach, be tough and aggressive as possible as you can, don't be sweet, like my cat don't have that mentality of trying to please everyone at your expense, I tell you this, in the long run you will command their respect and trust as they will look up to you as their role model they will also start solving their problems and becoming better people as well, in the future they won't hide behind you. a shoot now and ask questions later. Try to adopt

In my own experience, I have realized that humans unlike animals like the cat's, emotions and feelings play a major role and this in itself is a weakness and a major factor towards failures. Be as cold as can be if it's a friend hindering progress just avoid that friend without explanations and embark on your journey to achieving greatness. Don't be discouraged by others who will tell you that many have gone that road and failed, its true many people have tried and failed otherwise we all will be millionaires, believe that we are all different and there is one you and you are that one out of the million who will put their heads down and achieve greatness.

This book is to guide you by providing you with detailed sound and tried methods that if followed depending on one's self drive to excel, they will achieve their goal. It's the belief that you are that one person who will achieve what many have failed to achieved.

I had a friend of mine she was determined to succeed as well, she looked at different on-line business opportunities and researched a lot about starting her own clothing company, she went to these business starter centers and was bombarded with information that nowadays there were too many online businesses in her chosen field that it would be difficult to make it big time, in other words according to the jargon they used the market was flooded and any money invested was ear marked to be lost but she was that determined she believed she would fight competition and be the luckiest to steal customers from others and survive, she believed first she would make it in face of stiff competition and obstacles, she not only believed that she would make it she believed also that she was unique, she was oneself and not be generalized with the rest, she was that one person out of millions who will strike lucky and make it, she took the challenge to be competitiveness, dynamic and being a cut above the rest and this is exactly what it takes to survive in tough economic terms.

In most cases, it's that self-conviction as emphasized in previous chapters that one can make it, that self-realization and belief that you are You and therefore unique, you don't need to be stereotyped and be generalized. Don't stop doing what you want to try just because everyone else has failed.

Self-conviction is of crucial importance in all stages in order to be able to achieve greatness. I remember at Sunday school when I was a kid when the Sunday school teacher came to us and talked about a bible story when a man walked on water and another walked on fire. And as the teacher clearly explained.

The third man walked between hungry lions without being eaten. These stories were exciting and terrifying as well when we were kids, as you grow up you realize that these stories can be applied in our day-to-day life, they were like parables or paradigms which can help build us and make us take steps which society today consider impossible.

These are stories of faith, drive, ambition, determination, courage, persistence, resilience or a belief so strong to one that he or she believes that they can achieve their goal. Undoubted self-conviction that one can achieve greatness and that one is unique.

WRITE DOWN ANY IDEAS AND PLANS AS YOU GO.

1.
2.
3.
4.
5.
6.
7.
8.
9.
10.

Project to the time in the future when you have achieved your goal to keep yourself constantly motivated.

I'm not saying you can go in a cage full of hungry lions and not come out with your butt or limb missing. I'm just saying when it comes to making money or changing your lifestyle or achieving greatness.

Elina Salajeva

You need to believe that you can do what others cannot do, you must believe you have some kind of power and uniqueness. Metaphorically you can walk on water, all you need is self-conviction that you can do it and that it's you out of the million who can do it, and that its achievable regardless of the odds.

I remember some years ago when I was working at a farm in Germany, life was good, it was their busiest time of the year. The job was OK the first few weeks. This was farm work harvesting wheat and barley crops, we would wake up early in the morning going to the fields. The first few weeks were okay, it was something new to me, until that time I had never done work like this before. I had just left high school when I traveled to Germany.

It was great it was a new scenario, a new country and plenty of job opportunities but mainly in the farms. I was hungry for money, so there I find myself at a farm in one of Germany's countryside. We used to work long hours, we used to get up early in the morning going to work. We would work until in the afternoon then after that we take a break from the fields due to the high temperatures during midday. After a few hours when the sun was setting we would go back to the fields and work sometimes until 8pm at night.

No doubt the job was repetitive and routine working long hours but the money was great too. I was going to stay in Germany for a few months before I head back to Latvia my original country. It was great working in the countryside away from the polluted cities with car fumes everywhere, this was completely a different working environment, it felt good and uplifting, and refreshing, from far away you could hear the birds singing all day and wind slightly blowing and a cool breeze lingering everywhere. It was one afternoon, the sun was overhead, and it was near midday when temperatures are at their highest, when I sat on one of the combined harvesting machines and realized that I had been working long hours for weeks.

Chase Your Dreams Never Give Up!

I had started missing city life, a cup of cappuccino at the corner coffee shop, or a stroll to the cinema with my friend.

It was there and then when it heats me, I just realized that OK although the job paid very well, I just realized that I could be doing something much better with my life and getting the same money or even more. The job was ok but not just for me, I loved the countryside the beautiful scenery and the fresh air, I just realized that in the big city is where I belonged, I had to find a job that would pay better in the city but working just a few hours.

If possible, I would start my online business buying cheaper clothes and selling these at high prices online, or come up with my perfume line and market this. Growing up in Latvia Rezekne I had loved the sweet smell of different flowers and plants that one day I had wished I had my own perfume brand. Now if I get like a good startup capital, enough money to start my business, this could be one of the things I will look up at, I thought to myself.

It was there on this farm when I realized and believed that there was a problem which only myself had to address. It was up to me to set myself a challenge, to come up with a plan of how I was going to achieve greatness somewhere in the city. I had spent most of the time on the farm and most times in the fields, long unsocial hours and I was only 19. I started researching and brainstorming, I had that self-conviction that firstly there was a problem and that at my age I was destined to achieve great things, I knew I had a lot of potential, by this time I was fluently speaking five different languages Germany, Latvian, Polish, Russian and English.

I just knew it that somehow this was going to put me at an advantage, come competition or not I was prepared. I just knew it; this was the perfect moment to start taking control of my life making decisions that would turn my life around.

Elina Salajeva

Things that will make a life for me in the future fabulous. I just told myself that my ideal job would be a job where I work a few hours but earn a lot of money. On my lunch break that afternoon I went straight home unlike most lunch breaks where I would go to the canteen and spend time with my friends I worked with. Surprisingly that day I didn't feel like eating anything, my mind was full of ideas, I could picture myself in a big city office flicking a pen doing paper work rather than stuck in the wheat fields.

I could picture myself enjoying my job without having even a small drop of sweat. I went home sat down and took a small notepad, I started brainstorming, by the time it was time to go back to the fields, I had written down my detailed plan of how I was going to kick start my career. This job at the farm provided the money I needed to put my plans in place. I had no regrets working at this farm, sometimes in life it's taking odd jobs that makes you realize that you are destined for better things. This job not only provided the drive it provided as well the funds needed to lay the foundation of my career.

Today is the day of action, stand up and make that first step. Today say Yes I want this, draw plans today, calculate time constraints, calculate cost in terms of money, put dates and times when you can realistically start, buy or plan for everything needed, put in place things that makes this not just a onetime thing but a continuous improvement approach to a better you, to a better future, a better career, a better job, to a better lifestyle and to a new you in terms of how you look and feel about yourself. Look at personal and local influencing factors in relation to what you are trying to achieve, look at support from friends and family, look at relationships with loved ones and how this is going to impact on your progress.

Today is the day to take the challenge, don't just accepts the average, don't just go with the flow, be a trend setter, strive for the best, strive to be the best, aim higher and boost your self-esteem.

Take that challenge, convince yourself that you want this, and make that first move, take the challenge today.

Now I am going to look at the attributes you need to achieve your goals before I go into the methodology and guidelines for making your dream a reality. I explained in chapters above and as a recap, to me from my own experience as the title of the book clearly points out; Being, *tenacious, persistent, determined, steadfast, unswerving, diligent* and staying focused and on course until you achieve your goal is the most important thing if you are serious about achieving your goal.

First if you don't succeed, never give up pursue your dreams. Know what you want be fully determined, diligent and stay focused until you have achieved what you want.

Secondly you must be *fully determined and you must believe that a need exist, you must have the self-conviction that a need exist and that you really need this.*

You must take whatever you do seriously, set clear goals and you must believe that there is a problem and only then can you take everything serious and work towards a solution?

Thirdly, you *must aim higher, you must believe you can go beyond the ordinary, and to be unique you must be prepared to take risks.* It's doing what most can't do, it's going a mile further, taking risks as well that brings success.

Fourthly it's the *ability to take your opportunities, ability to recognize and anticipate these opportunities and have the confidence to take the opportunities with both hands* when they present themselves that distinguish success or failure.

Fifthly like explained above, you need good *leadership skills be your own boss, have the self-drive to do things your way.* Have the energy and drive and motivation to do well.

Have a clear vision of what you want to achieve have the energy and stamina and be resilient. You must have other qualities associated with leadership traits for example you must *make effective decisions, be straight to the point, be serious and make decisions regardless of feelings, be aggressive sometimes and say things as they are. Be truthful and strict.* All these will make you enjoy the rewards of your work in the future.

How to successfully set up your own business either online or establishing your own small business.

Firstly, I will look at how to successfully establish an online business. Online business is less risky you have fewer costs and you put less effort and the rewards can be great.

First you must identify a need in the market, do all your research find out what's missing and find out if you can fulfill the need. Sometimes it's identifying that niche market and targeting your business to those specific people and provide the service or goods they need. Do all your research, identify your targets, assess buyer behavior, assess competition, forecast sales and demand. Draw your business plans, know exactly what you want to do, in other words have clearly defined goals and put everything to plan

For some people, it's the gut feeling that drives you, it's the passion, confidence and drive and the belief that you can do it that see you through. You might not even worry about spending time researching and assessing demand and competition, you just get the basics of what you need to set up that business, from the ground taking risks as you go ahead creating this business. You must have the basics, knowing how much are your expenses and any other costs, you will need to look at all factors to successfully set up the business. The idea here is for you to try to do most of the big tasks by yourself. It's ok to find someone for example to design the website for you, but if you can do it yourself then the better.

It might not look great at first and improve it as you go along as the business grows, minimize initial costs until you start actually making sales and profits.

Do your research, find similar online businesses, learn from them see their business models, look at what they have done best, inherit what's good and tailor it to your own business model, always look for cheaper alternatives for example you might find out you will be able to sell most of your products but perhaps delivery costs will eat away all the profits.

Try to establish a good relationship with suppliers and everyone involved. The idea is to protect your profits at any cost. Always research, ask those who have been through this road, accept any help and use your own knowledge and experience to come up with cost-effective solutions.

This ability to protect your profits is the major key to the success or failure of your business. Most online business can make sales but some fail because costs eat away all the profits, storage and delivery to customers might be high that in the end it will be pointless to stay in business as all profits are lost.

This is the key area you must keep an eye on, do your homework, go beyond what everyone expects, go that extra mile, look for a cost-effective way of running your business, in most cases it's not the ability to sell a product or service as you can easily make sales but it's that drive to protect the profits that distinguish failure from success.

Like explained before write a sound business plan with clearly defined goals, register your domain name and set up your website. Test drive your website, make sure that there are no glitches involved make sure everything functions properly, and it's simple and ready to use.

Always at first strive to choose cheaper cost-effective ways of establishing your website ideally do it yourself. Take care of all the legal requirements in terms of data protection and compliance with other rules for instance, tax rules. Make sure your business is legal.

Make sure your website is working properly before advertising it but once it's running, then start spreading the word. Join twitter and Facebook as these are the most obvious social media to generate interest and awareness of your business. Start blogging find other effective methods of marketing your product and the more your business grows the more the sophistication your marketing method will be.

Rule number one

Don't waste time thinking about doing things or establishing the business, action now! Procrastinating is not good for any business, be quick to react don't be afraid to fail. In actual fact failing is part and parcel of starting your own business. People learn from mistakes; they take risks they don't wait for a time when things are right because there will never be a tight when conditions will be deemed as ideal. There is a lot of competition and it takes a lot of balls to jump in and in most cases, you might actually discover a great idea from a failure of an earlier attempt.

They say in business it's taking some guided risks that determines the success or failure of a business. Don't be afraid to make mistakes and don't let this fear stop you from starting your own business.

Rule number two.

Protect your profits at any cost otherwise you will be out of business. Look at all your costs, look at storage, assess all possible alternatives, look at transport costs and do the same, look at all other costs and do the same.

Look at forming good relationships or partnerships with suppliers, distributors and others involved to try to minimize your costs. Reduce waste, aim for right first time and always find better cost-effective ways of doing things. Look for cheaper e-commerce software packages for setting up your business and these should be your first choice and as the business grow then upgrade.

Be persistence never give up, look at all alternatives reduce costs be it overhead or after sales and in the future, this will pay off.

Rule number three

Work hard to establish viable networks with everyone involved from suppliers to distributors and above all have a strong bond and a view of the customer.

Without the customer, you would be out of business, the customer is of paramount importance. Have a good team that understands and values the customer because this is vital to the survival of a business. The business should be customer focused strive for exceptional customer service.

Rule number four.

Let the business grow first before you start taking money from the business. Many fall in the habit of taking loads of money from the business as soon as they start making a profit, this is bad for the survival of the business. Don't be greedy you might need more cash in the future as there might be some unforeseeable event in the future that requires cash injection. These businesses are easy to set up and with a lot of competition there might be the need for cash in the future for the survival of your business.

Rule number five

Make security be a priority you must protect your stock as well as customer information. Customers should feel secure and protected when they are shopping on your website. Choose a good e-commerce solution that has been tested and tried, with a good track record to protect your website and your customers from hacking and fraud.

Rule number six.

Be passionate about your business, have the drive and motivation to stay focused to make plans, redesign plans and make new plans. If you are passionate enough in selling clothes online for instance, that drive and passion will overcome any competition as you will become more creative and that passion encourages fresh thinking and innovation which puts competition at bay. Keep the fire burning don't just spend money on a project for instance, designing the website and then lose interest and fail to promote and advertise effectively to generate sales.

Don't leave everything to stagnant keep the spirit up promote your website through Facebook and twitter or start blogging about your business. Whatever it is the idea is to generate interest continuously reaching potentially new customers.

Rule number seven

Be realistic but optimistic set ambitious goals but achievable to some extent. Don't set big targets or have your sights unrealistically too high. Any forecast should be ambitious but achievable to keep the moral going otherwise a huge divergent from the results might dampen the spirit. Your calculations and forecasts should be based on facts and previous research, avoid over staffing or buying things like big storage space which you don't need, ideally stock items at home or a small storage facility and upgrade as the business grows.

Buy things you need now and as the business grows then expand and buy more as when needed.

Rule number eight.

Employ people who understand your business and what you are trying to achieve. Employ your staff based on their skills and qualities and not because they are your friends and relatives. Be strong and strict emphasize the need to view the customer as the sole existence of the business. Through training and development instill a culture where you provide and uphold excellent customer service. Motivate your staff and be strict and aggressive as well yet honest and predictable.

Put things in place to constantly motivate yourself and help you to keep focused and on the ball. Follow these guidelines and rules and take into considerations each step or issue raised. Missing one or ignoring one will impact how you will perform in the future.

WRITE DOWN ANY IDEAS AND PLANS AS YOU GO.

1.

2.

3.

4.

5.

6.

7.

If it's a new challenge, you want to make in terms of finding a new job with better remunerations and prospects look at the current situation. Take a small piece of paper write down what you think are the current problems right now, it could be poor wages or fewer opportunities for promotion or development. Look at your skills and experience. Research if the company you work for are offering other positions with better wages or remunerations. Ask the job specifications and requirements and compare this to your own skills and experience. Talk to managers about training and development. Ask the management if they can send you to do a course whilst still on the job. This should be your first point of research and inquiry.

Look at all the possibilities try to find out if you can do a private course, look at your means and time constraints and try to see if you can afford it. Look at all possibilities, there is no harm in researching to find out if something can be done.

The main purpose of this book is not to try to adjust the current situation BUT the emphasize here is on a complete change of the current situation, a complete change in direction, a complete change of a company or your employer, a complete new rewarding job. This should be the challenge the more the risk you take the more the rewards. It's about taking the risk, it's about taking a new direction, it's about saying no to the general norm, it's about getting out of your comfort zone. It's about chasing your dreams and never giving up. It's about going for that idea you had when you were a kid, an idea you had some years ago, that idea on plans gathering dust somewhere in the cupboard or garage. It's about realizing that the current job isn't for you no matter how good it is this moment in time it's not about paying bills, it's going beyond the idea of the comfortable living to the luxurious lifestyle.

It's about doing what you wanted to do as a kid, or something that completely overhauls your lifestyle. It's trying what you have ever wanted to do or what you have tried to do and failed. Did you ever wanted to be a musician, a doctor, a dentist, a stockbroker, a manager and so on? Depending on your age, or your personal circumstances this is still achievable. If you are young or old, the sky is the limit, take that challenge today say yes, put that plan in place, for some jobs this requires a lot of cash injection and don't let that stop you.

Do your research there are a lot of organizations and bodies that can fund you. Do your research ask a lot of people who have done similar jobs or courses and start planning? If this means saving some money and staying in your current job put plans in place, give yourself dates when you can realistically start. Look at other constraints and see if you can start after saving some money.

Switch to other jobs that provides a lot of money over short periods but with less long-term benefits to generate money to lay your foundation. Look at other alternatives like on the job placements, internships etc. The key here is research, ask a lot of people who have walked that road and make that first step. There are a lot of obstacles and frustrations, you must have the drive and will to continuously motivate yourself. You must be determined and be resilient to stay on course.

Have that self-conviction that you need this? Convince yourself that you want change and this is the only way you are going to achieve your dreams. If it's a course of study or training, then invest your money and time towards that. If you have to sacrifice something a car for instance, for some months whilst you do the training so be it, or sell a family caravan to raise the money you need to enroll on the course so be it. If you are determined and focused, if you are persistent and diligent then you are bound to achieve your goals.

Follow the above rules, they apply as well to you just tailor-make these according to your goals or what you want to achieve. Follow the rules and guidelines above. Look at yourself as a brand a product or service. Look at ways to improve yourself and esteem be it by improving your image, your skills or your knowledge. I have found it easy that learning another language can give you a competitive edge with the opening of the global job markets. You can easily outweigh competition and you will have a wide variety of job opportunities.

Learn a new skill, take a hobby to relieve the stress, connect to a social network, open a twitter account or Facebook account and share ideas and information. Make new friends with same goals, involve your family and friends and let them have some interests in what you are doing, that way you will have support in the long run.

Look at all the important factors mentioned above in previous chapters. Look at all the attributes you must have or inherit and follow the rules above, avoid procrastinating and minimize your costs, research and try to find cheaper ways and solutions of training, you can study at home or online and still get a good recognized qualification, establish good relationships, be your own leader, be your own boss, be your own source of motivation and drive, continuously strive to stay focused, give your studies your best efforts. Teach yourself to avoid mistakes because any failure can be a waste of time and money.

Put your head down for the duration of your training or study. Don't be nice to people who are not beneficial to you, keep the relationship only if it makes sense and you benefit from it. Don't stick around just because you must, let not your personal feelings cloud your judgment, if it's your friend slowing you down.

Taking your valuable time by taking you to the pub when you feel you should be studying or training then explain to your friend that you have no time for him or her if he or she doesn't understand then cut any links. If you stay on course continually applying everything mentioned in this book you are destined to achieve your goal.

I, myself has suffered from weight problems in the past. There is nothing wrong with being big, nothing wrong with being overweight I personally think this is one's choice of how they want to live their life. I'm speaking from my own personal experience I and I would argue that being overweight can be a problem. I missed on things like playing hobbies and sport at school because I was a bit overweight, I used to eat healthy but I am one of the few with genes that make your body grow quickly. I was finding it had to exercise because of my weight as a kid and as I was growing up. I was bit withdrawn from social networks I spent some time watching telly and in the house and missing socializing with my friends.

WRITE DOWN ANY IDEAS AND PLANS AS YOU GO.

1.

2.

3.

4.

5.

6.

CHAPTER NINE

At times, I had low self-esteem as I was often a target of bullying at school because of my weight. It was late in my teens after feeling sluggish and having a low self-esteem that I just knew that I had to do something about this. I just realized that I was accepting this situation of being overweight as something I was destined to be.

One day it just heats me I knew that I had to do something about this situation. I knew that it was up to me and no one else, it was myself who was to take that step in changing my life. I had that self-conviction that I had to do something. I knew time for action was now, I had to take control of things, start on a healthy living lifestyle, start exercising and training and watching what I eat and how I spent my time.

It was easy to motivate myself, I knew I had to say yes to a new me, I had to motivate myself and stay focused. I looked at my current situation, my eating habits, things I used to eat, my social environment and my networking with friends and other people. I took a post-it note and wrote down first what I thought was the main contributing factors before I did my research. I noted the major factors like fizzy drinks, I used to drink Pepsi one every day and the sugar content in it meant that, I kept piling on weight. I spent most of my free time studying.

If not academic stuff then it was learning a new language. I don't regret it because now I can speak five different languages Latvian, polish, Russian, English and Germany. I was not playing any sports or hobbies I knew I had to do something.

I did my research, I put a plan in place to make sure I won't go back to my comfort zone. I chose food I found out to be beneficial to me and eliminated all sugary foods and all fat foods. I realized it was not only about the food I had to get hooked on a hobby or sport to keep me on track and motivated. I had tried in the past to try to achieve my goal but after a few weeks of training I was back into my comfort zone. I had school commitments, I spent a lot of time at school and school stuff was taking a lot of my time.

I lacked persistence, I lacked the resilience and the stamina to keep on going. I gave up too quickly it was just unworkable. I knew this time I had to put things in place, I had to be very strict and true to myself if I had any chance of overcoming my obstacles. There was no room for being weak, I had to make tough decisions and put procedures in place so I don't go back to where I was. How did I fail last time? That was the first question that came into my mind. I tried to find out myself how things had started very well and why I ended up failing to achieve my goal. At first I was highly motivated, I remembered not feeling hungry the first days. I had that motivation to succeed, I wanted to look fabulous, I wanted to feel good about myself, I knew it was up to me to take the challenge.

In the past I, had changed my diet from the first day I instantly withdrew all the foods I thought were contributing to my problem it was an instant withdrawal but I later discovered that this instant withdrawal was a mistake as this contributed to my failure. This was due to lack of energy as I quickly got tired, instant withdrawal meant that I got hungry too quickly.

I had to change the way I go about it, I remembered telling myself. I knew for some food instant withdrawal wasn't the correct way because the last time I tried this I ended up running out of energy, I felt too tired and didn't have the stamina to keep pushing ahead.

All fizzy drinks, all sugary foods were first to go and all fast foods replaced with good high energy foods, I researched and introduced fruits that had high energy reserves like bananas. I introduced potatoes, rice, exotic foods and tried new foods as well. I had a plan in form of a calendar with dates and foods to eat as well as times to eat the food. In the past anytime was food time when I ever felt like eating I would just take food and eat. After researching I discovered that my eating habits were a big contributing factor. I used to eat at night after 10pm any fast food.

This time I knew I had to stop eating after a certain time at night.

My plan was in three parts first it was looking at food I was eating and their calories, secondly this was to do with what I was doing in my spare time and any social activities and thirdly I had to assess and look at a hobby or sport I was going to be hooked on as part of my healthy life style challenge.

The first part of my plan was to eat healthy foods, reduce all bad foods, fatty foods all processed foods, introduce new foods, new fruits and vegetables. The idea was not to starve myself. I changed my eating habits, I put a curfew on what time I should stop eating at night, I calculated how many times I should eat a day and adjusted this after every week. I didn't cut my portions drastically I slowly started eating less per session I spread my eating throughout the day.

I started eating with friends who ate less, friends who had the same goal as me.

Chase Your Dreams Never Give Up!

I knew if I had to make it this time I had to change or introduce new friends who are like-minded for support and motivation. I started reading weight watchers magazines to keep myself motivated, I started researching about people who had been through my situation, people who had already achieved their goal. This helped keeping me motivated and on track, I knew I had to keep the fire burning.

I noticed also that my sleeping habits were contributing to the problem as well. I had been sleeping very late at night waking up late as well when it's not school days. I used to wake up feeling tired from heavy meals I ate after 10pm. Eating at night contributed a lot to weight gain because after the meal I would go to sleep and the body stored all this food as fat as it had nowhere to put it. It was an eye opener; I knew I had to change a lot of my habits if I had to seriously do something about this situation.

Another thing I noticed was that I tended to put on a lot of weight near examination dates, I think due to stress and anxiety. I was producing more of the bad hormone cortisol which disrupted my metabolism, worrying was not a good thing too.

My plan included an analysis and breakdown of the time I spent on other activities that contributed to the problem. I spent most of my time studying at home or in the school library. This was a contributing factor to my weight as well, I had little time to do a sport or a hobby. I started allocating more time to spend outdoors, sometimes I would go and study to my friend's house which involved traveling to and from her house, I started exercising in my room allocating few minutes doing exercises or yoga. I started watching music that had dancing in it and started dancing too imitating what I saw in the videos.

The third part of the plan involved getting hooked on a hobby or something that would make me achieve my goal. I had started doing yoga which really helped me feel more relaxed but I knew this was not enough. I needed a hobby that required running, walking, jumping and more. Dancing to fast music was the first ideal choice I knew if I maintained a pattern and frequently danced to the music, I was going to achieve my goal. This really helped me the first few weeks but proved problematic as I felt really hungry afterwards that I would feel tired and drained. I laid down on my bed and thought of a plan that was going to work and make me achieve this. I realized that I had not visited my friends for some time who lived few miles away. I drew a plan in the form of a timetable with all my friends' address showing roughly how many miles to their house and what time I can visit them.

I knew that somehow if I make this regular this would not just boost my confidence spending time with friends but this was to help me overcome my weight problems as well. I would spend some hours a day traveling and walking and I would not think about food most of the time. Compliments from friends and advice from others might really motivate me I thought to myself.

I was nervous, but I knew that if I had to win my challenge, I had to spend time with people who had achieved what I was aiming to achieve.

I followed my plan, I started spending less time home, that in turn meant less eating, because sometimes I ate because I was bored I had nothing interesting to do. I spent time walking to and from my friends' house. After a few weeks, my confidence just grew up my self-esteem rocketed. For the weeks, I had been doing this I had not missed any visit, and I actually started doing even better at school. I started spending less time studying on my own studying with friends meant fast learning.

Chase Your Dreams Never Give Up!

I started eating with my friends, it was very beneficial as I started eating new foods and eating less.

My challenge was to visit at least five friends a day. This was like the hobby I got hooked up on since the day my friends first saw me they saw the transformation week by week and their compliments were a big motivating factor. Every week was different, I lost weight week by week and I started feeling better and better and looked fabulous after a few weeks. My friend's compliments from week to week made me want to keep on pushing ahead with my plan.

I looked forward each week to visit them so they can see an improved me week after week.

WRITE DOWN ANY IDEAS AND PLANS AS YOU GO.

1.

2.

3.

4.

5.

6.

7.

8.

9.

10.

Nothing wrong with being big and beautiful but if that stopping you from enjoying other things in life then it might be time to act.

So, a recap on the points and guidelines or things that one must follow to achieve their goal.

Like in the chapters above you must convince yourself that you want this change and you want this new healthy lifestyle. Without this self-conviction that there is a problem and you really want to do something about it there is a tendency of giving up.

The realization that there is a problem and a need to change current situation motivates one to do something about it and there is a need to continually keep your eyes on the ball. Persistence is of paramount importance there are so many problems and mistakes that makes one quit quickly.

The first problem one should try to avoid is regarding starving oneself. The main mistake which even I made on my first attempt was feeling so overzealous that one tends to cut out all energy providing foods instantly that in the end hunger strikes more often.

Instantly withdrawing most foods without replacing them with other foods will lead to hunger and failure.

The other problem is when portions a drastically reduced so fast that the body is starved and one ends up without energy reserves to carry on with the task at hand.

The third mistake is to remove all the food we are used to eating that in the end one feels deprived which in turn brings anxiousness that can make the body produce bad stress hormones. This can kill the willpower to stay focused.

The fourth problem is starting the process without any kind of measuring or of checking progress this can lead to failures. First collecting all statistics is important so you can measure progress in the future. Compliments from friends and relatives, measured weights, and the image you see in the mirror from day one are all important.

Not following a detailed plan and methodology and guidelines to achieve this can result in failures. Follow a detailed plan showing you all the things you must do for example how many hours you sleep a day, a reminder to drink water every day, recording data everyday all these contribute to your success.

Having looked at the above obstacles or mistakes here I'm going to write what is a guideline of successfully achieving one's goals based on my own experience.

First one must have the understanding that for most people being overweight can be a problem as you miss out on certain things in life because you can't do it you end up with low self-esteem. Missing on certain things which you would otherwise enjoy if you were not overweight will be your motivational factor and your drive to stay focused.

Write down what you are missing on a piece of paper and let these be your guidelines of what needed to be done. If it's a small size red dress, you saw on the window of the departmental store in town and the idea of rubbing your heaps on the dance floor with your friend excites you then let that be your drive. Whatever it is write it done picture it in your mind, actually buy that small size dress and display it in your room. If that actor with toned muscles, you want to look like then get his picture and stick it in your room.

Try to have the actual physical object you want, you are missing, you are craving to buy, so save money and buy the item even if you don't fit it yet.

After establishing that self-conviction and the casual effect relationship and believing yourself that you need this then can you only start the challenge. This is what you need to do to achieve your goal.

First look at the food you are eating and adjust your diet to include healthy foods. Don't stop eating the food you like but try to replace these with healthy foods which provided good vitamins and essentials. Switch to healthy fats like olive oil, and those found in avocados and fish. Reduce processed foods with a lot of sugars and opt for healthy unprocessed foods like fruits, vegetables and meat and fish.

Chase Your Dreams Never Give Up!

Avoid all calories found in fizzy drinks and confectioneries. Don't starve yourself just reduce your portions and spread your eating to 4 to 5 times per day eating small quantities. Drink a bottle of water every day to help your metabolism and to restore water lost during exercises.

It's not just about food, have enough rest and sleep as well. This is important and watch the time at night you eat. Ideally eat early and don't eat after 9pm.

Look at your social network and family settings and try to associate yourself with people who have achieved what you are trying to achieve. Spend time with friends who eat less. Keep your willpower high try to motivate yourself as described above.

Put things in place that will help you achieve your goal, include time to spend doing an exercise or a hobby. Go to the gym if you can afford it, took dancing lessons, dance to fast music at home, start yoga lessons, go outside to the park for a walk for sightseeing more often. Reduce time you spend at home where it's easy to just go in the kitchen and find yourself a big meal.

Get yourself hooked up on a hobby and for me this was the greatest must-do thing that helped me achieve my goal without reverting to my comfort zone.

The first time I tried it I lacked something I got hooked on and in the end, I failed. The second time I had a list of friends, their addresses, dates and times on a calendar this was the greatest weapon in fighting overweight for not only did I spend my time traveling this meant also spending less time at home where I'm surrounded with food, it meant a great deal of support, as the first days it was hey you still haven't lost that childhood weight to Waal you look amazing just a few weeks down the line. This boosted my morals, and I had something to look forward to. I had few friends before my challenge and

I ended up with a lot of friends I communicated with on a daily basis.

There are numerous other small things you can do to help yourself lose weight as above look at what you are doing right now and look at alternatives that involves some form of exercise for example if going upstairs at work you always take an elevator why not take the steps, why not walk the dog yourself instead of your partner, if you have food delivered why not go to the shops and collect the food yourself, if you watch your kids play why not play together with your kids. The idea here is to get involved and do things you normally don't do that involves any form of running, walking, jogging, etc.

This is not just about food and exercising it's about everything including reducing your worries and stress levels, this is about having something to look forward to, having the willpower to fight for what you want.. Be persistent and diligent. It's not easy but it can be achieved you need to understand the whole process and through a detailed tried and tested method only can you achieve this.

Think like my cat Persik, if he wants something be it food or a head-rub he won't stop mewing until he gets want he wants, whatever you want in life it's your will power stopping you, convince yourself about the current situation, the current problem and that you really want to correct this or achieve certain things and you have the stamina and willpower to do it then you can. I have put my methods to test and they worked for me, so why can't this work for you.

Don't accepts the norm this is not your destiny believe you can achieve greatness, start today take action make that move follow the guidelines above and take the challenge today. Chase your dreams and never give up.

Chase Your Dreams Never Give Up!

Chase Your Dreams Never Give Up!

Dream achieved but it wasn't easy, determination, resilience and sheer willpower enough to move mountains. Great days with friends.

Chase Your Dreams Never Give Up!

Chase Your Dreams Never Give Up!

The End

Chase Your Dreams Never Give Up!

www.ingramcontent.com/pod-product-compliance
Lightning Source LLC
Chambersburg PA
CBHW071034080526
44587CB00015B/2612